100
HISTORIC AIRPLANES
in Full Color

JOHN BATCHELOR

DOVER PUBLICATIONS, INC.
Mineola, New York

ABOUT THE AUTHOR

John Batchelor has been drawing aircraft, ships, tanks, and all things technical since he was four years of age—at least; his drawings collected by his mother during World War II prove this to be so. On being refused entry to art school, Mr. Batchelor went off and worked his way around the world, drawing many details of the ships he worked and traveled on. At eighteen years, he joined the RAF for his national service, filling further sketchpads in the process.

In January 2000, John Batchelor marked his fortieth year as a free-lance technical artist, working for many international publishers and specializing in "cutaway" illustrations. He also produces postage stamps for thirty-eight countries. Mr. Batchelor is a light aircraft pilot and fanatical fly fisherman—casting his flies in many countries. He is also a collector of "proper" jazz, and he carries a sketchbook wherever he goes. Apart from drawing, he is happiest driving tanks, and flying in any type of air-craft, going to sea in any type of ship, firing guns of all sorts, all of which comes within the remit of being a technical artist.

The author wishes to thank Malcolm Lowe for his invaluable help with the text.

JOHN BATCHELOR ILLUSTRATION: www.publishingsolutionswww.com

Copyright

Copyright © 2000 by Dover Publications, Inc.
All rights reserved under Pan American and International Copyright Conventions.

Published in Canada by General Publishing Company, Ltd., 30 Lesmill Road, Don Mills, Toronto, Ontario.

Bibliographical Note

100 Historic Airplanes in Full Color is a new work, first published by Dover Publications, Inc., in 2000.

DOVER *Pictorial Archive* SERIES

Library of Congress Cataloging-in-Publication Data

Batchelor, John H.
    100 historic airplanes in full color / John Batchelor.
        p. cm. — (Dover pictorial archive series)
    ISBN 0-486-41246-6
    1. Antique and classic aircraft—Pictorial works. I. Title. II. Series.

TL670.3 .B38 2000
629.133'34'0222—dc21

                                                              00-031775

Manufactured in the United States of America
Dover Publications, Inc., 31 East 2nd Street, Mineola, N.Y. 11501

Title Page Illustration: DE HAVILLAND DH.82 TIGER MOTH (plane no. 27)

Powered Flight: A Century Without Equal

The greatest adventure of modern man has been the conquest of the skies. It is almost impossible to imagine life in the 20th century without aircraft. And the farther we move through the century, the more remote becomes the idea of man without air travel. The earliest pioneers of flight—flying under balloons or in gliders—were regarded as cranks by most people, until the combustion engine was introduced into their inventions, making the balloon an airship and the glider a powered aircraft. After the Wright brothers' triumph at Kitty Hawk in 1903, many joined the rush to become airborne. World War I (1914–18) brought about enormous advances, including all-metal aircraft as large as some modern airliners. Between the wars, the architects of air power raced to develop better and faster engines and airframes for civil and military aviation. But it wasn't until the Second World War (1939–45) that the greatest technological advances took place, when the jet engine was tried and tested, and airframes became far more sophisticated in design and durability.

After World War II, there was a tremendous acceleration in the race for aeronautical supremacy in both civil and military fields. As many began to discover the pleasures of foreign travel, engineers developed bigger and faster aircraft with longer range capability to satisfy the growing appetite for long distance travel. In less than a century, what was at first available only to the privileged few is now enjoyed by millions from all economic strata. In 1919, the first airliner carried two passengers at 73 miles per hour; now one can travel at 1,350 miles per hour and at an altitude of 60,000 feet on a Concorde jet. Military aircraft can achieve much higher speeds and venture to the edge of space, reminding us that space travel itself was not possible until man first conquered gravity with the airplane. In the past century, there have been immense strides in fields such as medicine, communications, and other forms of transportation; but none have had a greater impact than powered flight, along with its technological breakthroughs that continue to have widespread application in many other fields of human endeavor. The future holds many exciting new possiblities for the world of aviation. New advanced fuels, revolutionary new designs, and the possibility of airplanes that travel into space all point to the conclusion that man's exciting adventure with aviation has only just begun.

—*John Batchelor*

WRIGHT BROTHERS' ENGINE OF 1903

The engine that ushered in the beginning of powered flight was a four-cylinder, water-cooled horizontal engine which produced twelve horsepower and weighed about 200 pounds.

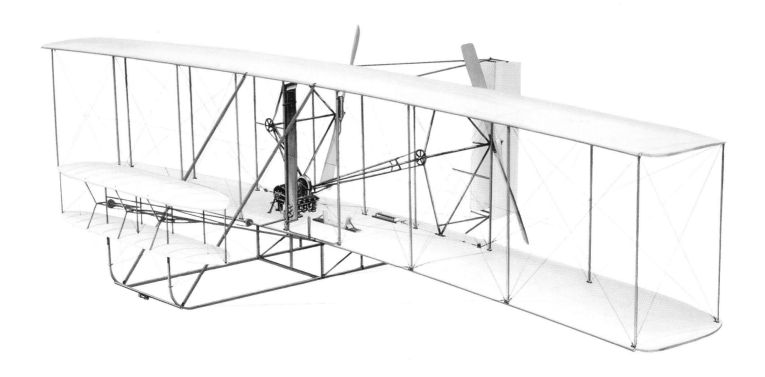

1. WRIGHT FLYER

Man's exciting conquest of the skies began on December 17th, 1903 when Orville Wright achieved the first sustained, controlled, and powered flight of an airplane near Kitty Hawk on North Carolina's Outer Banks. The momentous event came after many months of careful experiments in the completely new science of mechanical flight by the aviation pioneers from Dayton, Ohio, Orville and Wilbur Wright. The very first takeoff of the Wright Flyer biplane lasted for just twelve seconds and traversed a distance of about 100 feet. It was powered by a twelve horsepower engine built especially for this historic first aircraft; and in the days and weeks that followed, many longer and farther flights were attained. In 1905, the Wright brothers successfully designed and tested the first fully practical airplane. About four years later, they won a U.S. Army contract for the first military airplane. With their combined genius, passion, and persistence, the Wright brothers proved that man really could fly, and made heavier-than-air flying machines a practical reality.

2. LEVAVASSEUR ANTOINETTE

One of the early European pioneers of manned flight was the French engineer and boat builder, Léon Levavasseur, whose graceful Antoinette was one of the first practical monoplane designs. The series of Antoinette monoplanes that he inspired used wing warping—i.e., twisting the tips of a wing to preserve lateral balance—for the kind of control similar to that developed by the Wright brothers for their 1903 Wright Flyer biplane. The Antoinette helped introduce the concept of manned flight to Europeans, an idea that had already caught the imagination of Americans after the success of the Wright brothers.

3. BLÉRIOT TYPE XI

Frenchman Louis Blériot flew into the pages of history in July 1909 when he became the first person to fly across the English Channel, a feat considered incredible in its time. He piloted his own Blériot XI monoplane, with its innovative twenty-five horsepower Anzani radial engine, from the northern French coast to his landfall near Dover in southeastern England. Blériot won a £1,000 prize from the London *Daily Mail* for this historic thirty-seven minute flight, and his achievement made him a huge celebrity not only in his own country but around the world.

4. FARMAN MF.7 LONGHORN

Bringing the new art of manned flight within reach of many people was the achievement of the successful mass-produced biplanes of the Farman company in France. Among the most famous of their series of biplanes were the Farman III and the MF.7 Longhorn, so named because of its long outrigger "horns" that carried the front elevators. Henry Farman pioneered the use of ailerons—separate moveable control surfaces on the wings—which made the aircraft more efficient and easier to control than did the wing-warping system. The Longhorn was used to train many fledgling aviators, both in civilian life and for the military air forces that were created in many countries from around 1910 onwards. Longhorns also served as trainer and reconnaissance planes during the early part of the First World War.

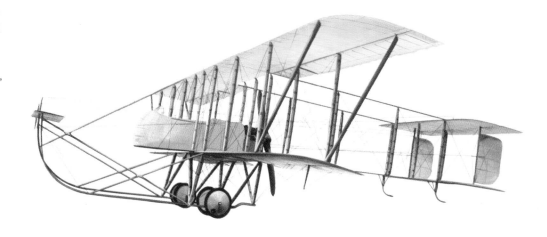

5. NIEUPORT 11

World War I was the first major war in which airplanes took part, and one of the most significant early fighter planes was the little French Nieuport 11—nicknamed "Bébé" (baby) due to its small size. Powered by a powerful and reliable Gnôme rotary engine, the Nieuport 11—initially designed as a racing aircraft—was developed into a fighter when the war began. One of the earliest mass-produced fighter planes, it was widely used early on by the British, French, and Italians. Some of the first pilots who became well-known fighter aces later in the war originally flew the Nieuport 11, engaging in legendary air battles with the monoplane Fokker E.I and E.III Eindecker fighters.

6. FOKKER E.I EINDECKER

The ancestors of the modern fighter plane—the monoplanes Fokker E.I and the later E.III—were possessed of an advanced design for their day. They incorporated such important technological advances as machine guns that could fire directly forward through the spinning propeller blades, instead of the inefficient upperwing-mounted guns found on some biplane fighters. An "interrupter" mechanism—linked via the engine to the propeller shaft–prevented bullets from striking the blades, thus allowing the guns to be aimed at the enemy much more accurately. In German service, the Fokker monoplane fighters were so successful in 1915 and early 1916 that a large number of British and French aircraft were shot down by what came to be known as the "Fokker scourge." Many successful German pilots like Max Immelmann and Oswald Boelcke became renowned for their exploits as fighter pilots in Fokker Eindeckers.

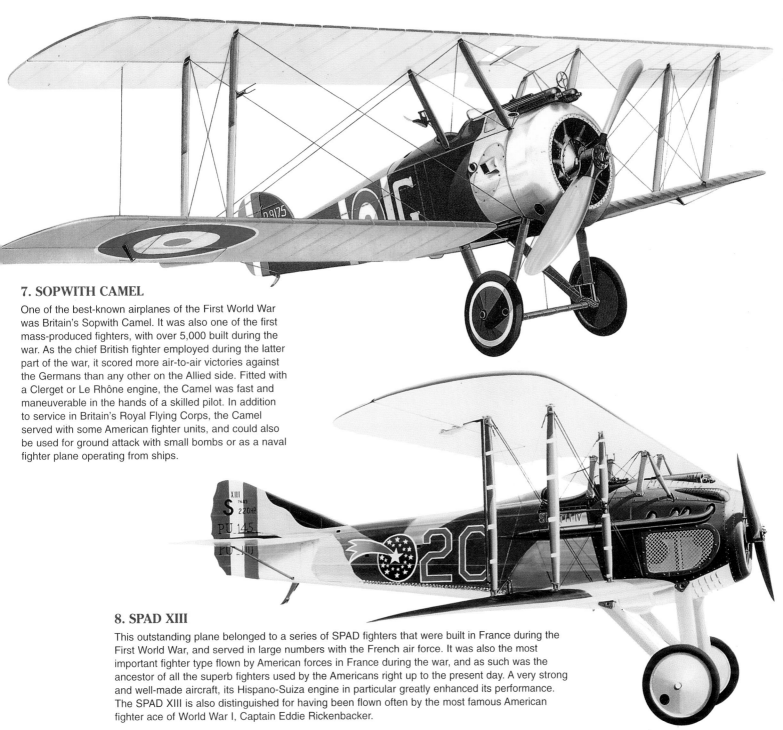

7. SOPWITH CAMEL

One of the best-known airplanes of the First World War was Britain's Sopwith Camel. It was also one of the first mass-produced fighters, with over 5,000 built during the war. As the chief British fighter employed during the latter part of the war, it scored more air-to-air victories against the Germans than any other on the Allied side. Fitted with a Clerget or Le Rhône engine, the Camel was fast and maneuverable in the hands of a skilled pilot. In addition to service in Britain's Royal Flying Corps, the Camel served with some American fighter units, and could also be used for ground attack with small bombs or as a naval fighter plane operating from ships.

8. SPAD XIII

This outstanding plane belonged to a series of SPAD fighters that were built in France during the First World War, and served in large numbers with the French air force. It was also the most important fighter type flown by American forces in France during the war, and as such was the ancestor of all the superb fighters used by the Americans right up to the present day. A very strong and well-made aircraft, its Hispano-Suiza engine in particular greatly enhanced its performance. The SPAD XIII is also distinguished for having been flown often by the most famous American fighter ace of World War I, Captain Eddie Rickenbacker.

9. ROYAL AIRCRAFT FACTORY SE.5a

Fast and strong, with excellent flying qualities, the SE.5 and SE.5a fighters built by Britain in the later stages of the First World War were among the finest Allied fighter planes of the conflict. Together with the Sopwith Camel and the SPAD XIII, they spurred the Allied victory over the Germans in 1918. Many British squadrons flew the SE.5a, and smaller numbers of the plane served with American units as well. Several famous British pilots—such as high-scoring ace James McCudden—became famous while flying the SE.5 and SE.5a, inspiring the legends of these heroic knights of the air that continue to be told even today.

10. JUNKERS J.1

The German Junkers J.1 was an all-metal monoplane that represented a significant advance in aeronautical design since—at that time—most planes were made from wood, with wire bracing and fabric covering. Making its first flight in late 1915, the J.1 was in many respects the ancestor of the all-metal monoplanes that would eventually succeed the wooden biplanes of the First World War era. The first in this family, the J.1, as well as some of its descendants, was nicknamed "Tin Donkey." Some of the later Junkers designs were used successfully in combat, where their metal construction made them nearly indestructible.

11. FOKKER D.VII

The best German fighter toward the end of World War I was the Fokker D.VII, also regarded as one of the finest biplane fighters of all time. Fast and maneuverable, with very good high-altitude performance, several high-scoring German aces flew this famous fighter plane. In fact, the Fokker D.VII attained the conspicuous distinction of being the only German airplane specified as booty by the Allies according to the surrender terms of the Armistice, impelling Anthony Fokker to smuggle his airplanes and factory contents out of Germany and into his native—and neutral—Holland. The planes continued in production there and were sold to many countries.

12. AVRO 504

Although the first Avro 504 flew in 1913 before the start of the First World War, this rugged biplane served throughout the war and continued in service afterwards, with over 10,000 produced. Primarily used for training thousands of airmen—first for Britain's Royal Flying Corps, and later for the Royal Air Force (RAF)—some of these planes were used in combat for reconnaissance and light bombing, and even as fighters. After the war, many Avro 504s were sold to civilian operators for everything from pilot training to barnstorming. Some were painted in bright colors by their civilian owners.

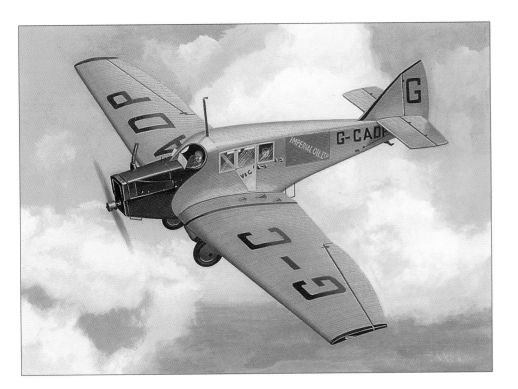

13. JUNKERS F.13

The Junkers F.13 was a descendant of the all-metal "Tin Donkey" aircraft that the German company created during World War I. First flown in 1919, it was both the first all-metal transport plane and the first aircraft specifically designed as a civilian airliner. The F.13 became very successful, with approximately 350 being built. With their strong, corrugated metal skin and ability to carry four passengers, this true ancestor of today's passenger transport planes played a significant role in the massive growth of air transport in Europe and in other parts of the world during the 1920s.

14. VICKERS VIMY

Occupying a key position in the history of aviation is Britain's Vickers Vimy. Designed in the latter part of the First World War as a bomber, the Vimy came too late to see service. Because of its excellent range and flying characteristics, it became useful after the war for long-distance flights. In June 1919, a specially adapted Vimy—with two 360-horsepower Rolls-Royce engines—made aviation history by being the first aircraft to fly non-stop across the northern Atlantic Ocean. The sixteen-hour flight of 1,890 miles was made by two intrepid British aviators, Captain John Alcock and his navigator, Lieutenant Arthur Whitten Brown. The two won a prize of £10,000 from the *Daily Mail* and were knighted by King George V for this singular achievement. Not only did their accomplishment make the world seem like a smaller place, but it also suggested the viability of commercial passenger flights across the north Atlantic in the future.

15. BOEING PW-9

Among the first major fighter types designed in America and ordered into service for the U.S. military in 1925, was the long line of fighters produced by Boeing in the 1920s with the designation PW-9. "PW" stood for pursuit (fighter) with a water-cooled engine. This series of fighters served with the U.S. Army in such distant destinations as Hawaii and the Philippines. The U.S. Navy also ordered their own versions of this successful early example of American fighter design.

16. CURTISS R3C

The sleek, streamlined Curtiss R3C seaplane was a real champion. One of the fastest biplanes ever built, it was specially designed to participate in an important international air race known as the Schneider Trophy. The purpose of this competition was to help aircraft designers of the 1920s and 30s produce ever faster and more powerful machines. Flown over the triangular course of seven laps for a total of 217.5 miles by the renowned U.S. Army pilot Lieutenant Jimmy Doolittle, the Curtiss R3C won the Schneider Trophy race in 1925, shattering all existing seaplane records at a speed of 232.6 miles per hour.

17. FOKKER F.VII-3m

The 1920s and 30s were great pioneering times in aviation, when new air routes were established, and inaccessible parts of the world were visited and explored by intrepid explorers in all shapes and sizes of aircraft. The three-engined Fokker F.VII-3m—the world's first tri-motor—gained fame in 1926 when it was used by American explorers Lieutenant Commander Richard E. Byrd and co-pilot Floyd Bennett on the Byrd Arctic Expedition. In this plane, the two pioneers successfully located and flew over the North Pole, which was one of the most inaccessible parts of the world up to that time.

18. BOEING F4B

Fast and agile, the Boeing F4B was an important U.S. Navy fighter of the late 1920s and early 30s, representing one of the most advanced examples of the biplane fighter design when it entered service. The U.S. Army also ordered this little Boeing fighter, which became known as the P-12 in Army service. Boeing F4Bs were powered by the classic Pratt & Whitney Wasp air-cooled radial engine, which was one of several important aircraft engines made in the U.S. from the 1920s and 30s onwards.

19. RYAN NYP

Today we take for granted the ability to fly great distances across the world's oceans in modern airliners, but in 1927 the idea of flying across the northern Atlantic Ocean was still a daunting prospect. Although several people like Alcock and Brown had by then successfully managed to do so, no one had yet made a solo flight. That is, not until May 1927, when American Charles Lindbergh became the most famous person on earth for flying non-stop across the North Atlantic from New York to Paris, France. Lindbergh's aircraft for this epic achievement was the American-built Ryan NYP, the "Spirit of St. Louis," and custom-made for Lindbergh at a cost of just $6,000. The heroic flight took over thirty-three hours and thirty minutes to complete.

20. BOEING MONOMAIL

The Boeing Model 200 Monomail, which debuted in May 1930, represented a new era in high-speed mail and passenger transport, as well as the future trend in American transport plane design. Its revolutionary features included a beautifully streamlined airframe and a retractable undercarriage. These all-metal monoplanes were powered by a 575-horsepower Pratt & Whitney Hornet radial engine, and could carry six passengers over an unrefueled distance of 575 miles at a cruising speed of 135 miles per hour.

21. NORTHROP ALPHA

Considered an epoch-making plane for its time, the Northrop Alpha of 1930 was a streamlined, all-metal, stressed-skin monoplane that could carry six passengers at a time. It was part of an important series of early yet sophisticated airliners, the Alpha/Gamma/Delta series, designed by famed aircraft engineer, Jack Northrop. The ancestor of the Douglas DC-3 passenger planes, the Alpha was the harbinger of things to come, signalling the end of the days of the biplane.

22. BOEING 247

A direct descendant of the beautifully streamlined Boeing Monomail mail carrier, the Boeing Model 247 was one of the first modern American airliners of the 1930s. With its all-metal construction, cantilever wing, and retractable landing gear, this twin-engine monoplane was the result of Boeing's experiments to create a revolutionary airliner layout. The first Model 247s entered service in 1933, and marked the beginning of a new era in air transport—offering clean, fast, air-conditioned service for its passengers.

23. HAWKER FURY

Just as the Boeing F4B and P-12 represented the peak of biplane fighter design in the U.S., the sleek and powerful Hawker Furies were their British counterparts. This superbly engineered fighter first entered service in the early 1930s with Britain's RAF; it was further refined as the High Speed Fury, this model entering service with the RAF from 1936. Some of these airplanes were still in service at the start of the Second World War, by which time they had been almost completely replaced by the new breed of faster monoplane fighters.

24. SUPERMARINE S.6B

After American ace Jimmy Doolittle took the Schneider Trophy in 1925 with the Curtiss R3C biplane seaplane, the competition was won in following years by fast, advanced monoplane seaplanes made in Britain. The most important of these was the Supermarine S.6B, winner of the contest in 1931, and flown by Flight Lieutenant J. N. Boothman. The S.6B was designed by R. J. Mitchell, the brilliant aircraft designer who later designed the legendary Spitfire fighter.

25. PIPER CUB

There are few trainers and light aircraft that can claim to have the same success story as the Piper Cub. Once the exclusive province of the rich, this little tandem two-seater brought the possibility of flying to everyone who was interested in mastering the skill. Thousands of Americans learned to fly at the controls of a Piper Cub in the 1930s and 40s, and over 14,000 civil and 5,700 military examples were built. They were followed by a developed version—the Super Cub—itself an excellent training aircraft.

26. LOCKHEED ELECTRA

The Lockheed Model 10 Electra was a fine example of the modern, streamlined all-metal airliners with retractable landing gear which were produced in the United States during the 1930s. The company was founded in 1912 by three Irish brothers—born "Loughead"—who after a lifetime of being miscalled "Loghead," finally decided to change the spelling to match the correct pronunciation of their name, i.e., Lockheed. The Electra became especially famous because it was used by one of the great heroines of the skies, Amelia Earhart, in her attempt at an around-the-world flight in 1937. Unfortunately, this effort ended in failure when her plane disappeared over the Pacific Ocean, a tragic illustration of the kind of dangers faced by all early aviation pioneers.

27. DE HAVILLAND DH.82 TIGER MOTH

The little biplane Tiger Moth trainer was to the British what the Boeing Stearman was to the Americans. Captain Geoffrey de Havilland—the plane's designer—had other interests besides aviation, notably butterflies and moths, a fact which accounts for its name. It first flew in 1931, and many of its kind had already served civilian owners and flying schools prior to becoming the RAF's primary trainer before and during the Second World War. Thousands of trainee pilots learned to fly at the controls of a Tiger Moth before graduating to Spitfires; and it was also used for training pilots from many other Allied countries during the war. Well over 7,000 Tiger Moths of all kinds were built. Large numbers of these planes survived the conflict to return to civilian flying in the late 1940s and 50s.

28. FOCKE-ACHGELIS Fa.61

This unique machine was an early attempt to create a fully controllable vertical take-off and landing plane which would nowadays be called a helicopter. To combat the problem of torque, it had two rotors mounted on lateral outriggers. In fact, the Fa.61 was not like the modern helicopter as we know it, but was an important step on the road to its creation. First flown in Germany in June 1936, it was often demonstrated by the superb German female test pilot, Hanna Reitsch.

29. BOEING 314

The Yankee Clipper was the name of the first of the huge Boeing Model 314 flying boat series that gained lasting fame in 1939 when it realized the long-held dream of commercial flight across the Atlantic between North America and Europe. The airliner had a wingspan of 152 feet, and was able to carry up to seventy-seven passengers in its later form. It was the largest and most luxurious transoceanic airliner of the period. In the service of Pan American World Airways, the Boeing 314 established the commercial air routes over the Atlantic Ocean that still exist today—bringing Europe within one day of the United States. The plane also pioneered many other long-distance air transport routes over the Pacific Ocean. During the Second World War some of the Model 314s were put into military service where they proved as safe and reliable as in their operations for commercial airlines.

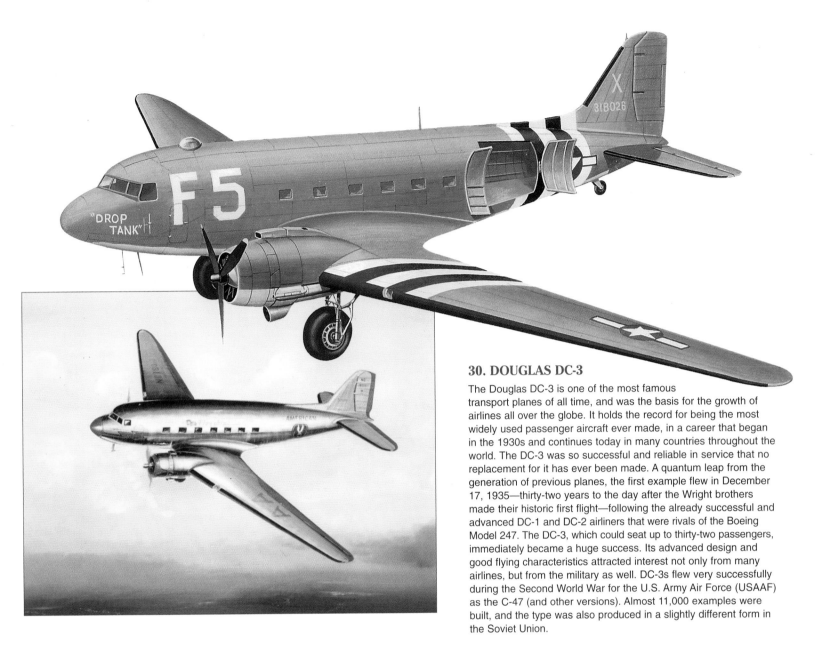

30. DOUGLAS DC-3

The Douglas DC-3 is one of the most famous transport planes of all time, and was the basis for the growth of airlines all over the globe. It holds the record for being the most widely used passenger aircraft ever made, in a career that began in the 1930s and continues today in many countries throughout the world. The DC-3 was so successful and reliable in service that no replacement for it has ever been made. A quantum leap from the generation of previous planes, the first example flew in December 17, 1935—thirty-two years to the day after the Wright brothers made their historic first flight—following the already successful and advanced DC-1 and DC-2 airliners that were rivals of the Boeing Model 247. The DC-3, which could seat up to thirty-two passengers, immediately became a huge success. Its advanced design and good flying characteristics attracted interest not only from many airlines, but from the military as well. DC-3s flew very successfully during the Second World War for the U.S. Army Air Force (USAAF) as the C-47 (and other versions). Almost 11,000 examples were built, and the type was also produced in a slightly different form in the Soviet Union.

31. BOEING STEARMAN

From 1936 onwards, U.S. military pilot trainees were taught to fly in one of the classic military training planes, the Boeing Stearman. Sometimes called Kaydet in USAAF service, Stearmans became the standard trainer not only for aspiring American military pilots, but also for those of other nations who received instruction in the U.S. and Canada during the Second World War. The Stearman's rugged biplane design was perfect for novices because of its excellent flying qualities, thus facilitating the move to the more advanced monoplane fighters and bombers then entering into front-line service.

Spitfire Prototype

Cockpit, Spitfire 1A

Supermarine Seafire

Spitfire IX

32. SUPERMARINE SPITFIRE

Surely one of the best-known of all fighter planes, the legendary Spitfire was the top British fighter of the Second World War. In fact, it was one of the few aircraft of any type to serve continuously right through the war—from 1939 to 1945. It was produced by the British aircraft company Supermarine, founded in 1912 by Noel Pemberton Billing, whose own personal view about true seagoing aircraft was reflected in the company's motto: "Not an airplane that will float but a boat that will fly." The Spitfire was designed by R. J. Mitchell, who had also designed the Schneider Trophy-winning Supermarine S.6B.

The first Spitfire flew in 1936, and all the early models were powered by the famous and powerful Rolls-Royce Merlin engine. The Spitfire and its companion the Hawker Hurricane were victorious in the Battle of Britain during 1940. In the years that followed, the basic Spitfire design was developed for fighter-bomber work. A special version for Britain's Royal Navy—called the Seafire—was also produced, with folding wings for stowage aboard ship. Many Spitfires were also flown successfully by the USAAF in Europe and North Africa. Later in the war a more powerful engine, the Rolls-Royce Griffon, was fitted to some Spitfire models to improve performance. These aircraft could carry up to eight machine guns in their wings, or a combination of machine guns and cannons. After the Second World War, Spitfires remained in service until they were replaced by some of the early jet fighters.

Spitfire MK.XII

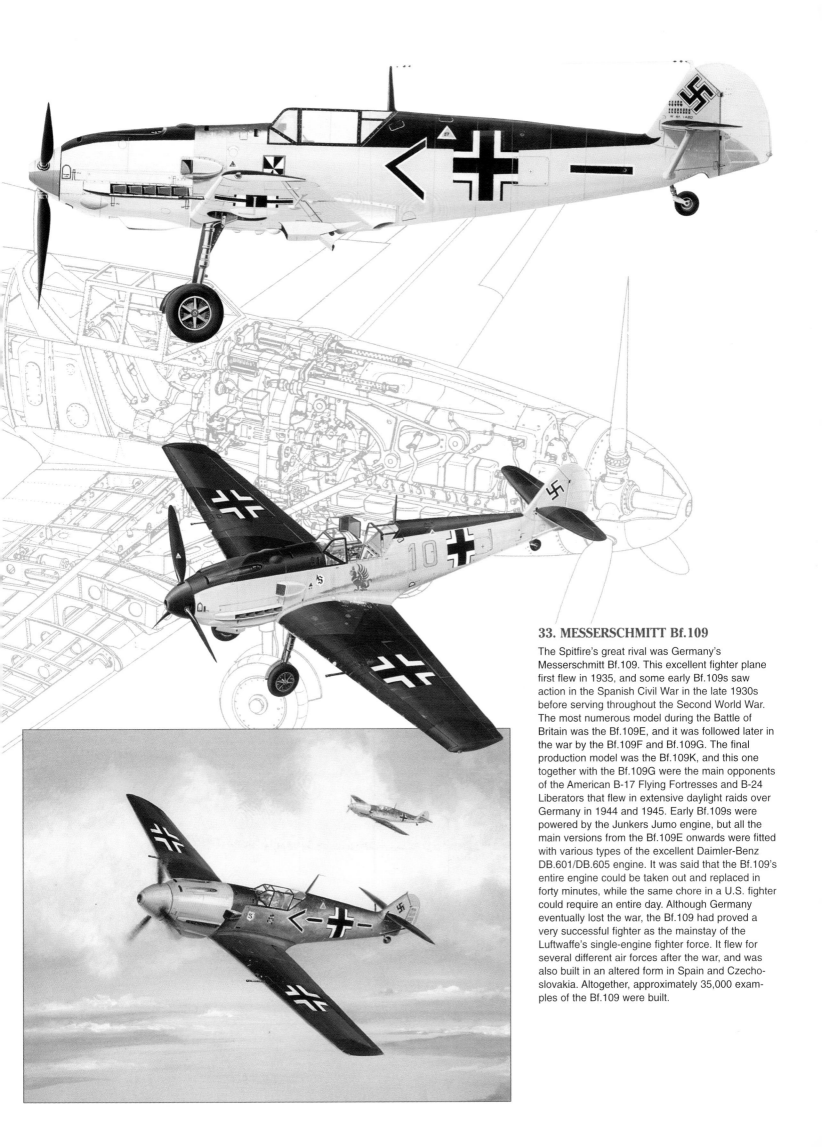

33. MESSERSCHMITT Bf.109

The Spitfire's great rival was Germany's Messerschmitt Bf.109. This excellent fighter plane first flew in 1935, and some early Bf.109s saw action in the Spanish Civil War in the late 1930s before serving throughout the Second World War. The most numerous model during the Battle of Britain was the Bf.109E, and it was followed later in the war by the Bf.109F and Bf.109G. The final production model was the Bf.109K, and this one together with the Bf.109G were the main opponents of the American B-17 Flying Fortresses and B-24 Liberators that flew in extensive daylight raids over Germany in 1944 and 1945. Early Bf.109s were powered by the Junkers Jumo engine, but all the main versions from the Bf.109E onwards were fitted with various types of the excellent Daimler-Benz DB.601/DB.605 engine. It was said that the Bf.109's entire engine could be taken out and replaced in forty minutes, while the same chore in a U.S. fighter could require an entire day. Although Germany eventually lost the war, the Bf.109 had proved a very successful fighter as the mainstay of the Luftwaffe's single-engine fighter force. It flew for several different air forces after the war, and was also built in an altered form in Spain and Czecho-slovakia. Altogether, approximately 35,000 examples of the Bf.109 were built.

34. VICKERS WELLINGTON

The Vickers Wellington was a formidable British bomber and anti-submarine aircraft of the early years of the Second World War. What made the plane unique was the unusual "geodetic" construction of its fuselage, consisting of a metal structure of diagonal interlocking members that made it extremely strong. This feature allowed many Wellingtons to return safely to their bases with battle damage that would have downed conventionally constructed aircraft. The first Wellington flew in 1936, and some examples of this medium bomber were still in service at the end of the war.

35. HAWKER HURRICANE

Although it never garnered the glory that the Supermarine Spitfire always enjoyed, Britain's Hawker Hurricane was nevertheless a very important fighter in British service. During the decisive Battle of Britain in 1940, the sturdy but slower Hurricanes actually shot down more German planes than did the nimbler Spitfires. The Hurricane first flew in 1935, and after the Battle of Britain it served as a cannon-armed fighter-bomber not only in Britain, but in many other theatres of battle.

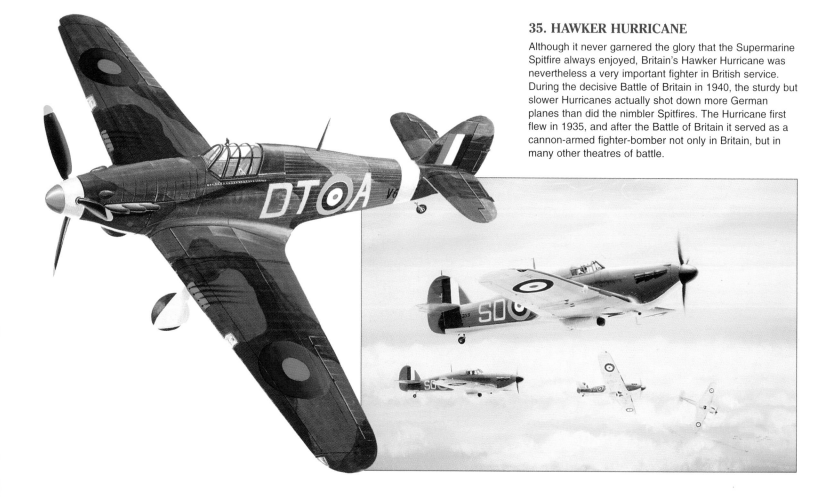

36. MITSUBISHI A6M ZERO

Japan's best-known combat plane during the Second World War was the Mitsubishi A6M Zero—code named "Zeke" by the Allies. This exceptional radial-engined fighter was the crowning achievement of Japanese design, gaining the Mitsubishi company a mark of distinction in the field of light construction. Early reports of its speed, maneuverability, firepower, and range were so incredible that American aeronautical experts passed them off as inaccurate—i.e., until the Japanese attack on Pearl Harbor on December 7, 1941, when a deadly aerial assault that included forty-five Zeros made these reports a grim reality. The plane served until the end of the war in a variety of different versions. Its prototype first flew in 1939, and almost 11,000 examples of this effective fighting machine were built. Toward the end of the war, Japanese kamikaze pilots crashed their explosive-filled Zeros onto enemy ships.

37. JUNKERS Ju.87

One of the big successes of the early part of the Second World War was the Junkers Ju.87 Stuka dive-bomber, which helped the Nazis defeat Poland and France. This aircraft played a key role in the German idea of "Blitzkrieg" or lightning war, in which planes like the Ju.87 coordinated their activities with ground forces to make very swift advances against the enemy. Designed to be a terror weapon, many were equipped with shrieking sirens for psychological effect. The first Ju.87 flew in 1935, and in action the Stuka would usually carry two crew members and a large bomb under its fuselage, dropping it at the end of a fast dive from a high altitude. The Ju.87's success story came to an abrupt end in the Battle of Britain, when they were easily shot down by Spitfires and Hurricanes.

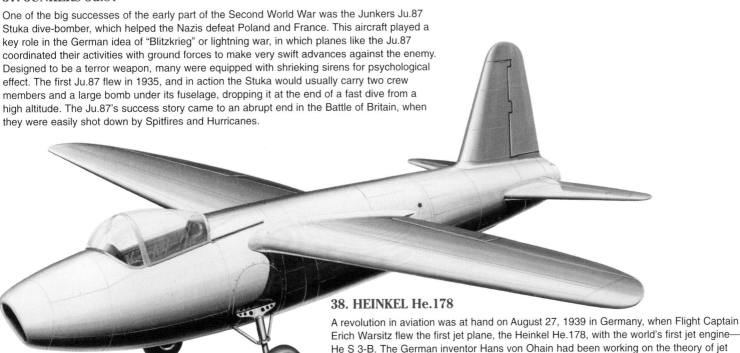

38. HEINKEL He.178

A revolution in aviation was at hand on August 27, 1939 in Germany, when Flight Captain Erich Warsitz flew the first jet plane, the Heinkel He.178, with the world's first jet engine—the He S 3-B. The German inventor Hans von Ohain had been working on the theory of jet propulsion for some time, and his experiments resulted in the successful flight testing of this single-seat research craft with monocoque aluminum fuselage. Around the same time, several other countries had made progress in the design and development of jet engines, but the Germans were the first to actually fly an aircraft with this entirely new type of power plant.

39. NORTH AMERICAN B-25 MITCHELL

On April 18, 1942, Lieutenant Colonel Jimmy Doolittle led sixteen B-25 Mitchell medium bombers on a daring air raid against Japan. All aircraft reached their targets. Launched from a U.S. Navy aircraft carrier—the U.S.S. Hornet—the "Doolittle Raiders" bombed Tokyo and other industrial centers, bringing a real morale boost to the United States at a time of great pessimism for the Allies during the Second World War. Doolittle was already famous for his win in the 1925 Schneider Trophy race flying a Curtiss R3C. The B-25 Mitchell was one of the best medium bombers of the Second World War. It first flew in 1940, and could carry around 3,000 pounds of bombs plus several forward-firing machine guns for strafing attacks.

40. JUNKERS Ju.88

The primary German medium bomber of the Second World War was the versatile Junkers Ju.88. Designed in the late 1930s as a fast tactical bomber with a crew of four, the Ju.88 served the German air force throughout the war in a variety of roles that included dive bombing, reconnaissance, and anti-shipping missions. Later in the war, some versions were fitted with radar to serve as night fighters operating against British night-bombing raids over Germany. Almost 15,000 Ju.88s of all types were built.

41. AVRO LANCASTER

It was the Avro Lancaster—Britain's best-known heavy bomber during World War II—that brought the war to the enemy in the form of many daring night raids, deep into the heart of Germany itself. Lancasters could carry a mighty bombload of up to 18,000 pounds in some versions; and close to the end of the war, some dropped huge bombs of up to 22,000 pounds—known as a 10-tonner "blockbuster"—on special targets such as bridges, viaducts, and warships. Several specially converted Lancasters carried a clever device called a "bouncing bomb," which was used to destroy several important German dams in the Moehne, Eder, and Sorpe valleys to flood factories and halt industrial production. Some Lancasters were powered by the famous Rolls-Royce Merlin engine.

42. BOEING B-17 FLYING FORTRESS

The most famous U.S. heavy long-range bomber of the Second World War was the Boeing B-17 Flying Fortress. This four-engined plane was best known for its daylight raids against industrial targets in German-occupied Europe, where epic air battles were fought against defending German fighters like the Messerschmitt Bf.109. Eventually the B-17s were escorted to their targets by P-51 Mustangs and other Allied fighters, but all the Flying Fortresses were piloted by brave young men, some of whom were barely twenty years old. When the first B-17 was flown in 1935, it was almost defenseless against fighter attacks; but a succession of different versions led to the B-17G later in the war—equipped with a total of thirteen Browning machine guns and carrying a ten-man crew.

43. FOCKE-WULF Fw.190

The technically advanced Focke-Wulf Fw.190 was an excellent German fighter that proved to be a big success when it entered combat in 1941–42, particularly against the Spitfire Mk.V, one of its chief opponents of the time. Powered by a BMW radial engine, the Fw.190 was also a very capable fighter-bomber; and later in the war it also served as a night fighter. An astonishing total of approximately 20,000 Fw.190s of all types were produced during the wartime period.

44. DE HAVILLAND DH.98 MOSQUITO

Nicknamed the "Wooden Wonder," the de Havilland Mosquito fighter-bomber and night fighter was an outstanding success with the British and American aircrews who flew it. Unlike most other warplanes which were fabricated from metal structures, the Mosquito was unique among the major World War II combat aircraft in being constructed almost entirely from wood. Even so, the plane was strong and able to withstand considerable battle damage. The first model flew in 1940, and in addition to its duty as a fighter-bomber and night fighter, the Mosquito could also perform reconnaissance missions, a role it continued to play after the war was over.

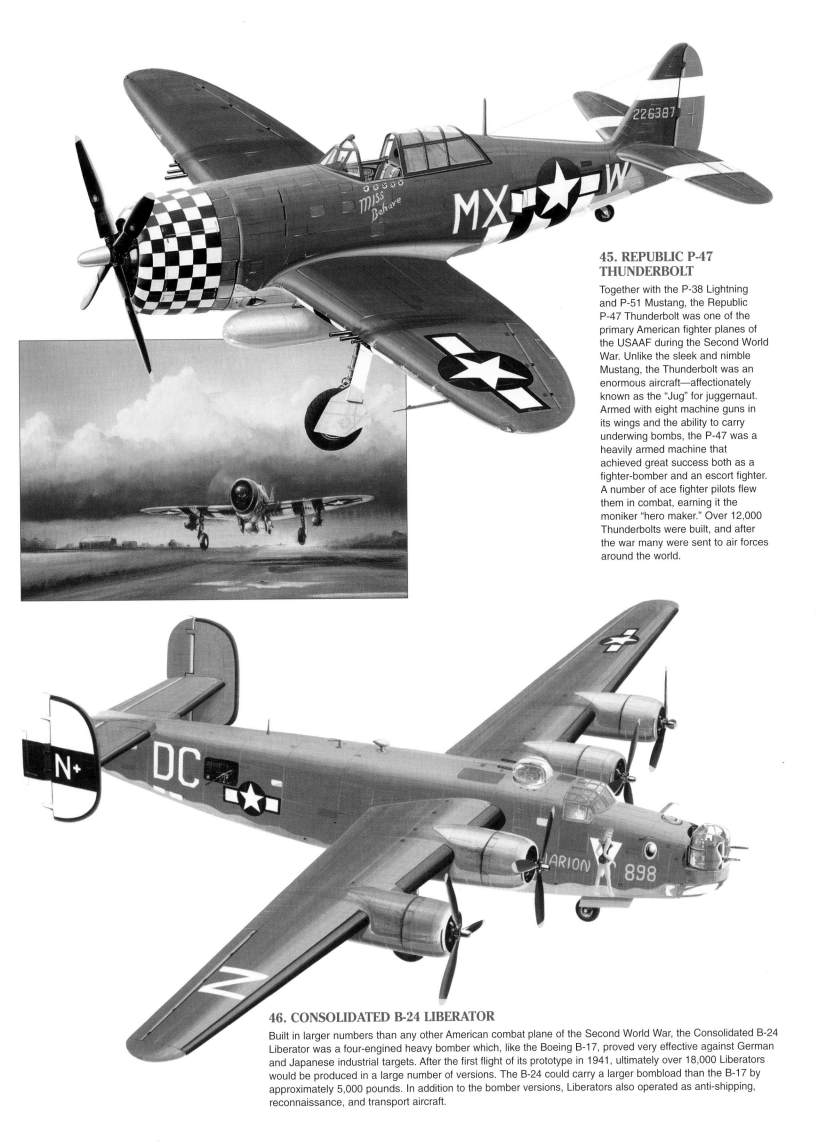

45. REPUBLIC P-47 THUNDERBOLT

Together with the P-38 Lightning and P-51 Mustang, the Republic P-47 Thunderbolt was one of the primary American fighter planes of the USAAF during the Second World War. Unlike the sleek and nimble Mustang, the Thunderbolt was an enormous aircraft—affectionately known as the "Jug" for juggernaut. Armed with eight machine guns in its wings and the ability to carry underwing bombs, the P-47 was a heavily armed machine that achieved great success both as a fighter-bomber and an escort fighter. A number of ace fighter pilots flew them in combat, earning it the moniker "hero maker." Over 12,000 Thunderbolts were built, and after the war many were sent to air forces around the world.

46. CONSOLIDATED B-24 LIBERATOR

Built in larger numbers than any other American combat plane of the Second World War, the Consolidated B-24 Liberator was a four-engined heavy bomber which, like the Boeing B-17, proved very effective against German and Japanese industrial targets. After the first flight of its prototype in 1941, ultimately over 18,000 Liberators would be produced in a large number of versions. The B-24 could carry a larger bombload than the B-17 by approximately 5,000 pounds. In addition to the bomber versions, Liberators also operated as anti-shipping, reconnaissance, and transport aircraft.

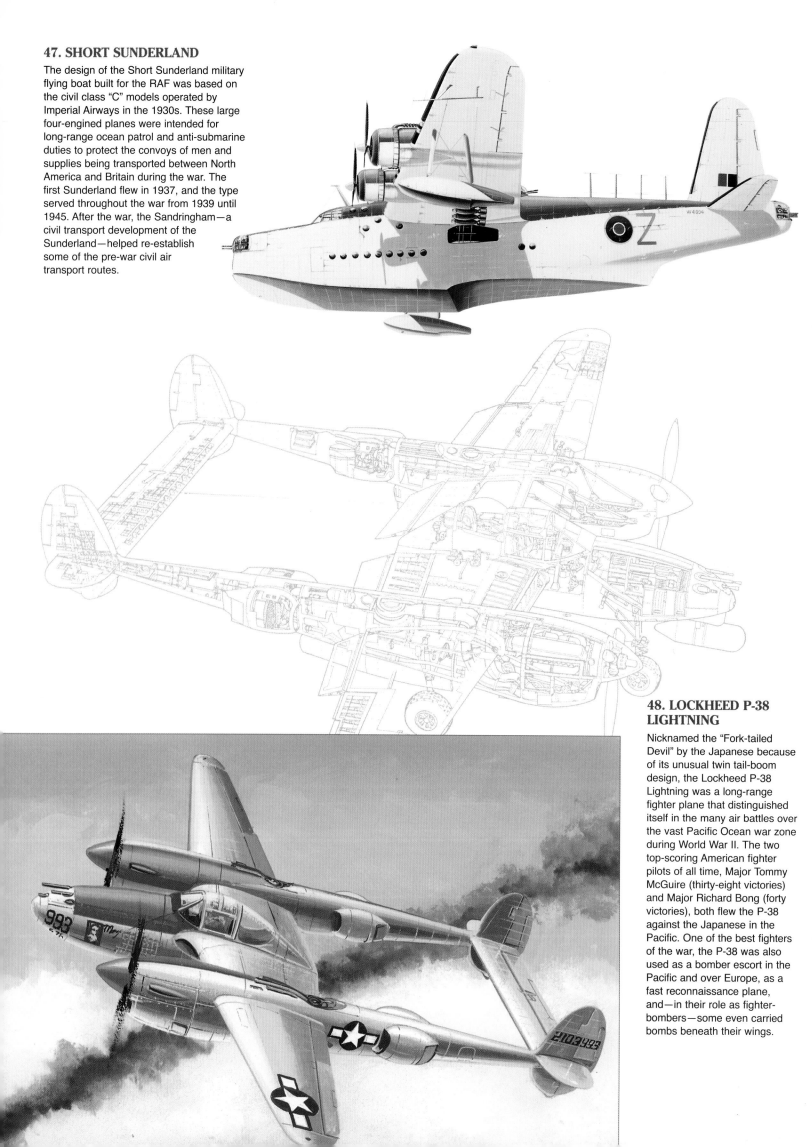

47. SHORT SUNDERLAND

The design of the Short Sunderland military flying boat built for the RAF was based on the civil class "C" models operated by Imperial Airways in the 1930s. These large four-engined planes were intended for long-range ocean patrol and anti-submarine duties to protect the convoys of men and supplies being transported between North America and Britain during the war. The first Sunderland flew in 1937, and the type served throughout the war from 1939 until 1945. After the war, the Sandringham—a civil transport development of the Sunderland—helped re-establish some of the pre-war civil air transport routes.

48. LOCKHEED P-38 LIGHTNING

Nicknamed the "Fork-tailed Devil" by the Japanese because of its unusual twin tail-boom design, the Lockheed P-38 Lightning was a long-range fighter plane that distinguished itself in the many air battles over the vast Pacific Ocean war zone during World War II. The two top-scoring American fighter pilots of all time, Major Tommy McGuire (thirty-eight victories) and Major Richard Bong (forty victories), both flew the P-38 against the Japanese in the Pacific. One of the best fighters of the war, the P-38 was also used as a bomber escort in the Pacific and over Europe, as a fast reconnaissance plane, and—in their role as fighter-bombers—some even carried bombs beneath their wings.

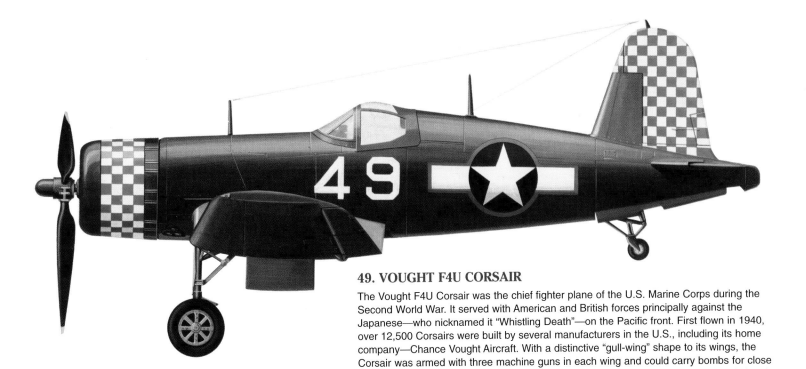

49. VOUGHT F4U CORSAIR

The Vought F4U Corsair was the chief fighter plane of the U.S. Marine Corps during the Second World War. It served with American and British forces principally against the Japanese—who nicknamed it "Whistling Death"—on the Pacific front. First flown in 1940, over 12,500 Corsairs were built by several manufacturers in the U.S., including its home company—Chance Vought Aircraft. With a distinctive "gull-wing" shape to its wings, the Corsair was armed with three machine guns in each wing and could carry bombs for close support missions in aid of ground forces. This aircraft also served with distinction during the Korean War (1950–1953), scoring ten aerial victories for the U.S. Navy and Marine Corps.

50. HAWKER TYPHOON

Purpose-built from 1940 onwards for fighter-bomber operations in support of friendly ground forces and against enemy troop concentrations and vehicles, the Hawker Typhoon proved a formidable opponent of German forces in France after the liberation of Europe was begun by the Allies in 1944. Powered by an enormous and sometimes troublesome Napier Sabre engine, the Typhoon made a vital contribution towards the final Allied victory over Germany in 1945. It flew mainly with Britain's RAF, and its main armament was a selection of underwing unguided rockets that were a very powerful weapon against enemy tanks and other vehicles.

51. GRUMMAN F6F HELLCAT

The top U.S. Navy carrier-based fighter plane during the Second World War was the large and powerful Grumman F6F Hellcat, originally a redesign of the Grumman Wildcat, built to accommodate the huge Pratt & Whitney Double Wasp radial engine. Incorporating combat lessons in its design—some of which were gleaned from a crashed Mitsubishi Zero in the Aleutians that was resurrected for study—it out-performed the Japanese plane in every category, and was credited with downing 5,000 enemy planes in all. The first Hellcat flew in 1942, and by the end of the war a large number of them were in service aboard the massive fleet of U.S. Navy aircraft carriers in the Pacific. Several famous fighter pilots and high-scoring aces flew the Hellcat, including Captain David McCampbell who scored no less than thirty-four aerial victories.

52. NORTH AMERICAN P-51 MUSTANG

The best fighter plane of the Second World War was the North American P-51 Mustang, thought by many to be the best propeller-driven fighter of all time. This magnificent machine served with the highest honor during the war with both the USAAF and the RAF, and contributed significantly to the Allied victory in the air war against Germany and Japan. The Mustang was developed in 1940 by North American Aviation, Inc. at the urgent request of the British, with the first model being produced at breakneck speed in 117 days. Early Mustangs were powered by an Allison engine and had good low-level performance. They were used by the RAF for reconnaissance and ground support missions, strafing trains, troops, and enemy installations at low altitudes.

After proving its worth in combat for the RAF, the USAAF became interested in the Mustang. When the American-produced Rolls-Royce Packard-built Merlin engine replaced the Allison, the Mustang's performance at all altitudes was immediately improved, and in that modified form the P-51 became famous. The best model was the P-51D shown here in various views, with three machine guns in each wing and an all-around clear vision cockpit canopy. Many famous fighter pilots flew the Mustang, and in its role as an escort fighter for B-17 Flying Fortress and B-24 Liberator heavy bombers, it scored many air-to-air victories.

53. YAKOVLEV YAK-9

Produced in large numbers, the Yak-9 was the finest Russian fighter of the Second World War. It belonged to the Yakovlev family of fighters that helped defend the Soviet Union against the Germans from 1941 until the end of the war. The first Yak-9s flew in 1942, and several leading Russian fighter pilots operated this agile and capable fighter plane in combat. The Yak-9 was also famous because it was used by French volunteers who fought alongside the Russians against the Germans, until they were able to return to France when the war was over.

54. BOEING B-29 SUPERFORTRESS

The American bomber that can truly be said to have won the Second World War was the mighty Boeing B-29 Superfortress. This heavy bomber was used in large formations in the later stages of the war to carry out major air raids on Japan. The B-29 was the first aircraft ever to employ remote-controlled power-operated gun turrets, and was the only Allied airplane that was large enough to carry the newly developed atomic bomb. In August 1945, two atomic bombs were dropped by Superfortresses: the "Enola Gay" flew "Little Boy" to Hiroshima and the "Bockscar" dropped "Fat Boy" on Nagasaki, propelling Japan's surrender and the end of the war, and officially ushering in the atomic age.

55. MESSERSCHMITT Me.262

With conventional propellers and piston engines replaced by jet propulsion, the Messerschmitt Me.262 was the most advanced jet aircraft of World War II. This unique airplane first flew in 1941 without jet engines installed, and had its first true jet flights in 1942. Finally, after a long development period, it entered service in 1944. In addition to a fighter-bomber version, there was another model built that was especially effective as a night fighter against American heavy bombers on their missions over Germany. Unfortunately for the Me.262, however, there were not enough examples of this revolutionary aircraft in service to make a decisive difference in the air war over Germany. And in several cases, the jet-powered Me.262s were caught by the slower P-51 Mustangs and shot down. Nonetheless, the Me.262 holds a very special place in the history of aeronautics as the world's first operational jet fighter.

56. GLOSTER METEOR

Although there was much development work on jet engines in Germany, some of the most important research was done in Britain. Frank Whittle, Squadron Leader of the RAF, had studied the possibility of jet propulsion for many years, and had started work on a gas jet turbine engine in 1929. The result of this research was the Gloster Meteor jet-powered fighter, which first flew in 1943 and entered service in 1944. The Meteor's service entry was roughly simultaneous with the German's jet-powered Messerschmitt Me.262, but the two never met in combat. After the war's end, the Meteor went on to become the most important British jet fighter for several years; and eventually, radar-equipped night-fighter versions were also produced.

57. LOCKHEED P-80 SHOOTING STAR

The first jet-powered aircraft to serve with the USAF, the Lockheed P-80 Shooting Star entered service in 1945 (although two examples were actually in active service in the war zone when the war ended). Designed to counter the enemy jets appearing in skies over Europe, the Shooting Star was built in just 143 days. It went on to become the most important American fighter in the years immediately following the war, and was redesignated the F-80 in 1948 when the USAF changed the lettered prefix "P" for "Pursuit" to "F" for "Fighter." This plane served with great distinction during the Korean War from 1950 onwards in both fighter and fighter-bomber roles, where it was credited with shooting down the first enemy MiG. Some P-80s were also used for reconnaissance; and a two-seat trainer version was developed as the T-33, serving for many years after the P-80 was finally withdrawn from service.

58. LOCKHEED CONSTELLATION

First flown in 1943, the Lockheed Constellation began its life as a military transport plane. However, after the end of the Second World War, when public demand for air transportation skyrocketed, the Constellation became famous as a civil airliner. This graceful plane re-established many pre-war air routes, and pioneered new ones with the aid of its excellent performance and long-range capabilities. Constellations that could accommodate forty-eight passengers entered commercial service in 1946 with Pan American and TWA. The years that followed saw the development of larger and more capable versions, eventually leading to its final incarnation as the seventy-five passenger Starliner.

59. BELL MODEL 47

The first really successful mass-produced helicopter was the Bell Model 47, which first flew in 1945 just after the end of the Second World War. Eventually over 5,600 were built in the United States, Britain, Italy, and Japan, and they were widely used by both civil and military operators. The 47D-1 version had a top speed of 98 miles per hour, and included Bell's patented stabilizer bar which made it the smoothest model to date. The triumph of this little Bell machine established the helicopter as an important and useful air vehicle; and the relatively low cost of owning and operating one allowed many people to experience the then wholly new concept of helicopter flight.

60. DOUGLAS DC-4 AND DC-6

Two key airliners in the re-establishment of civil aviation following World War II were the Douglas DC-4 and DC-6. The DC-4 was a pre-war commercial transport plane, whose four-engined military version saw distinguished service during the war—making flights and carrying loads far in excess of its designed capacity. As civilian airlines began to flourish after the war's end, the passenger form of the DC-4, along with the later, larger and more powerful DC-6, (shown below) marked a new era in air travel. Many of the early 52-seat DC-6s and later 107-seat models continued in service into the 1980s, and some even into the 1990s.

61. VICKERS VISCOUNT

During the Second World War civil aviation almost ceased to exist, and re-establishing commercial passsenger services at the war's end represented a formidable task. One of the most important airliners of the post-war years, the Vickers Viscount helped Great Britain reassert its role as aircraft supplier to the world. It was the first passenger plane to make use of a new type of engine called a turboprop (a gas turbine akin to a jet engine but propeller-driven), and about 450 examples of it were built up to 1964. Both European and American airlines jockeyed for position on the Viscount delivery line, since it was considered the height of luxury at that time to fly in the rear of this quiet, almost vibration-free passenger craft and be plied with champagne by a stewardess. Some Viscounts were still in use during the 1990s.

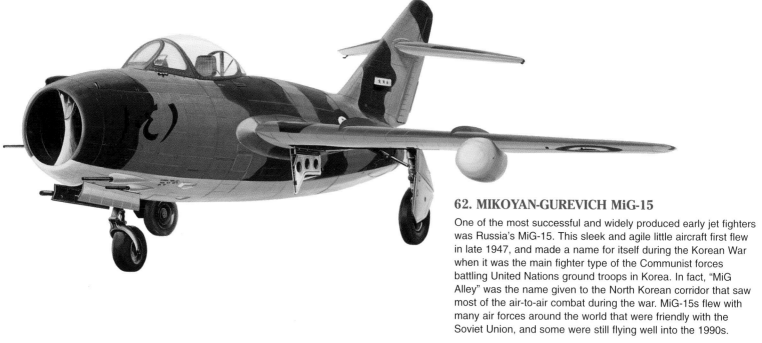

62. MIKOYAN-GUREVICH MiG-15

One of the most successful and widely produced early jet fighters was Russia's MiG-15. This sleek and agile little aircraft first flew in late 1947, and made a name for itself during the Korean War when it was the main fighter type of the Communist forces battling United Nations ground troops in Korea. In fact, "MiG Alley" was the name given to the North Korean corridor that saw most of the air-to-air combat during the war. MiG-15s flew with many air forces around the world that were friendly with the Soviet Union, and some were still flying well into the 1990s.

63. NORTH AMERICAN F-86 SABRE

The magnificent North American F-86 Sabre was a rugged and agile fighter plane which became famous for its exploits during the Korean War. The world's first successful swept-wing jet—with leading-edge slats for low-speed flight (a key feature adapted by engineers from a "liberated" Messerschmitt Me 262)—it was the only jet to distinguish itself in air combat. In the skies over Korea, USAF F-86s came up against the nimble little MiG-15, and some epic dogfights resulted. The American Sabres were flown by some very able pilots who eventually achieved a kill ratio of better than ten MiGs to every one Sabre. Most F-86s at that time were armed with six machine guns in the forward fuselage, but later versions were equipped with a radar nose for night interception duties, and rockets instead of machine guns.

64. HAWKER HUNTER

Great Britain's best jet fighter of the 1950s was the Hawker Hunter, which served with the RAF in large numbers. It was also a big export success, achieving robust sales in many foreign countries. Powered by the outstanding Rolls-Royce Avon turbojet engine, the first Hunter flew in 1951, and eventually almost 2,000 Hunters were built in all versions. This supersonic jet served with distinction in several wars, and broke the world air speed record in 1953. With the sleek and superbly balanced lines of its airframe, many aviation historians consider the Hawker Hunter to be the most beautiful aircraft ever built.

65. BOEING B-47 STRATOJET

The first all-jet strategic nuclear bomber to serve with the USAF's Strategic Air Command (SAC) was the big and impressive Boeing B-47 Stratojet, which first flew in 1947. Powered by six turbojet engines mounted in pods below its narrow swept-back wings, the B-47 was the most important military aircraft of its era, fulfilling SAC's mandate during the 1950s to maintain peace for the free world through nuclear deterrence. Approximately 3,000 Stratojets were built; they could carry up to 20,000 pounds of weapons, and sometimes needed a boost via JATO—Jet (actually rocket) Assisted Take Off.

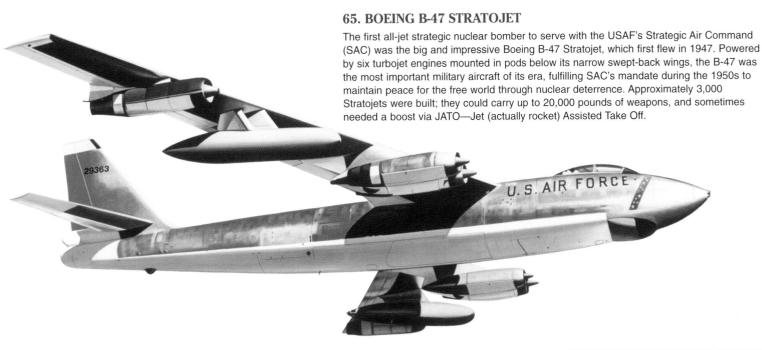

66. ENGLISH ELECTRIC CANBERRA

The outstanding English Electric Canberra was one of the best jet-powered medium bomber and reconnaissance planes ever produced, and it served with great success in many air forces all over the world. The first Canberra flew in 1949, and all production models were powered by two powerful Rolls-Royce Avon turbojets. It has the distinction of being the only combat aircraft with wooden parts–the forward part of the fin was made from plywood. Many special adaptations of this warplane were built, including attack-bombers which carried up to 8,000 pounds of bombs, reconnaissance and electronic warfare versions, and aircrew trainers. They were so popular, in fact, that the type was built under license as the Martin B-57 for the USAF, and were recalled from use by Air National Guard units for first-line service as strike bombers during the Vietnam War.

67. DE HAVILLAND DH.106 COMET

The modern era of jet-powered civil transport was inaugurated in May of 1952 when Britain's de Havilland Comet airliner, in the colors of the British Overseas Airways Corporation (BOAC), began regular passenger service from London to South Africa. The beautifully sleek four-engine jet, with a cruising speed of about 475 miles per hour, was the world's most advanced airliner at that time, and could carry around thirty-six passengers. Its chief American rival was the Boeing 707, and together these two passenger airliners changed the face of civil aviation.

68. CESSNA 150

The Cessna 150 was one of the classic light aircraft of the post-World War II era, when the aircraft industry geared up to sell planes to pilots who had learned to fly during the war. The two-seat Model 150 first flew in 1957, and several thousand were built for civilian customers in the U.S. and overseas. As a basic trainer, the Cessna 150 has brought the possibility of flight within the reach of many aspiring civil and military pilots who began their flying days at the controls of one of these fine planes.

69. BOEING 707

The first major American jet-powered commercial airliner was the legendary Boeing 707, the design that established Boeing as "plane maker to the world." Two years and 16 million dollars in the making, this remarkable four-engined plane first flew in July 1954. And although Britain's de Havilland Comet was already then in passenger service, the Boeing 707 went on to eclipse it and—in its many variations—become one of the world's most popular and successful jet aircraft for both civilian and military use. By the mid-60s, the 707 and other jets were replacing piston-engine liners; and ten years after Pan Am's inaugural 707 flight from New York to Paris in October 1958, orders for Boeing jetliners totalled nearly 2,000. Some Boeing 707s are in service even today, mainly on cargo operations; and there are many military models of the basic Boeing 707 design that are also still in widespread use.

70. AVRO VULCAN

The world's first delta-wing bomber, the Avro Vulcan really made the ground shake on take-off with its four huge Olympus turbojet engines at full power. Originally designed to an RAF specification for an aircraft that could deliver nuclear weapons from any of its bases in the world, the Vulcan formed a part of Britain's nuclear forces in the 1960s. It could carry several types of nuclear weapons or 22,000 pounds of conventional bombs. In the 1982 war between Britain and Argentina over the Falkland Islands, the Vulcan flew successfully for Britain, carrying conventional weapons.

71. DOUGLAS A-1 SKYRAIDER

The large and powerful Douglas A-1 Skyraider was designed as an attack plane for operations based aboard aircraft carriers. In 1946–47, the first Skyraiders entered into service for the U.S. Navy, and were very effective in their intended role during the Korean War in the early 1950s. A decade later, USAF-operated Skyraiders were an even bigger success in operations during the Vietnam War, where they were the best tactical ground-attack airplane available. A developed version with a huge radar dish fitted under the fuselage for detecting enemy aircraft was used by Britain's Royal Navy.

72. BOEING B-52 STRATOFORTRESS

The awesome Boeing B-52 Stratofortress is powered by eight jet engines, and is the most powerful strategic bomber ever built. It first flew in 1952, and became the USAF's chief long-range nuclear bomber. With a bombload of nuclear missiles or bombs, or up to 44,000 pounds of conventional (non-nuclear) bombs in its internal bomb bay and on external wing pylons, it replaced the B-47 Stratojet in service, and continues in front-line action today. B-52s carried out bombing missions during the Vietnam War in the 1960s and early 70s, and served again during the Persian Gulf War in 1990–91.

73. ENGLISH ELECTRIC LIGHTNING

In its time, the high-performance English Electric Lightning was the most formidable interceptor-fighter ever built. This large, sleek British aircraft entered service with Britain's RAF in 1960. With a top speed of over 1,500 miles per hour, the Lightning was armed with large air-to-air missiles designed especially for intercepting heavy bombers. For over a decade, it served in an air defense role for Britain in successively upgraded versions.

74. BELL UH-1 HUEY

The most widely used military transport helicopter of all time is the famous Bell UH-1 Huey, which first flew in 1956. Many thousands were produced for the American armed forces, as well as the air forces of many foreign countries. Up to seven armed troops could be transported inside the fuselage, and guns and even rocket packs could be carried by this aircraft. Hueys became especially famous for their performance during the Vietnam War, and some of the later production models are still in service today. Special gunship versions of the Huey with a redesigned fuselage have been developed for attacking tanks and other armored vehicles.

75. NORTH AMERICAN F-100 SUPER SABRE

The success of the F-86 Sabre led its manufacturer, North American Aviation, to design a developed model that could reach supersonic speed, and so the classic F-100 was born. This beautifully sleek and very fast fighter and fighter-bomber was the first of the distinguished series of American fighters known as the "Century Series" due to the F-100 designation of its first member, the Super Sabre. The first F-100s entered service in 1954, and fighter-bomber versions of this great warplane served effectively during the Vietnam War in the 1960s.

76. SUKHOI Su-7 FITTER

This successful jet fighter-bomber was the first member of a large family of Russian close air-support attack planes produced by the Sukhoi design bureau. The first example flew in the mid-1950s, and it went on to become the standard tactical ground-attack fighter for the Soviet Union. Fitters were the primary Russian-operated fighter-bombers during the 1960s, with thousands being exported to all Warsaw Pact nations, as well as to other pro-Soviet countries throughout the world.

77. DOUGLAS DC-9

The Douglas DC-9 was one of the finest medium-range jet airliners ever produced. With no less than 976 production examples built from the mid-1960s onwards, the basic DC-9 design also marked the beginning of a family of medium-range jetliners made by Douglas' successor, McDonnell Douglas, numbering from the MD-80 and MD-90 onwards. Some versions of the DC-9 could seat up to 125 passengers. Overall, these planes had an impressive service record with many of the world's great airlines.

78. BAC/AÉROSPATIALE CONCORDE

The Concorde—a joint British and French creation—was the first supersonic airliner ever to enter regular passenger service, and British Airways and Air France continue to operate this remarkable civil transport plane to this day. In regular service since 1976, the Concorde can carry up to 144 passengers. Its most distinctive feature is its unique hinged nose which tilts downward to improve pilot visibility for takeoff and landing, while for supersonic flight, the nose swings upward. The aircraft is powered by four huge Olympus turbofan engines and attain speeds over Mach 2—a level usually associated with the top speed of a supersonic fighter plane. Due to heating of the airframe, the 204-foot fuelage stretches up to ten inches in supersonic flight. Although there have been many plans over the years to replace the Concorde with a new generation of far bigger and faster supersonic airliners, the prohibitive costs have so far prevented them from becoming a reality. (Concorde views include the two below, as well as the two bottom illustrations on the facing page.)

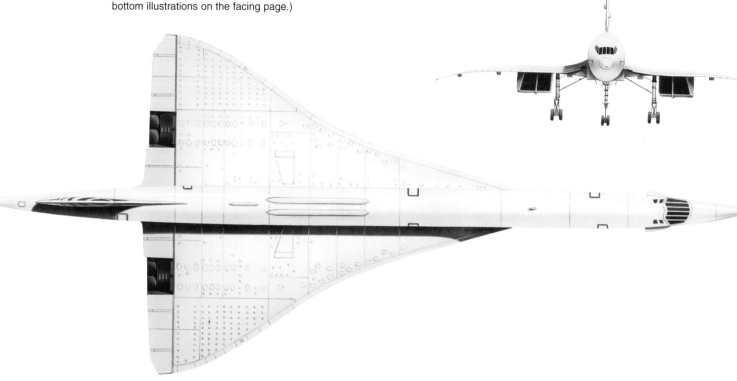

79. BOEING 747

Better known by its nickname "Jumbo Jet," the world-famous Boeing 747 is one of the most successful airliners of all time. In the early stages of production, manufacture of this behemoth had to be delayed so that Boeing could build a new forty-three acre facility at Paine Field, Seattle, one large enough to accommodate what would become the premier subsonic airliner. The first example was finally rolled out on September 30, 1968. The first 747s entered service with Pan American World Airways in early 1970, and its basic design has been progressively developed into more advanced and more powerful versions. Some Boeing 747s are configured specially as freighters, while others are equipped with special modifications to give them greater range. In some models, up to 516 passengers can be carried, depending on which one of the many alternative seating arrangements is used. Well over 1,000 747s have been built, and production still continues in Boeing's factories. The "Jumbo Jet" represents a true embodiment of the dream of air travel as pioneered by the Wright brothers.

80. LOCKHEED F-104 STARFIGHTER

Over 2,000 Lockheed F-104 Starfighters were built in America and several other countries like Canada and Japan. They also became an important fighter-bomber in the air forces of many western European nations. Nicknamed the "Manned Missile," the Mach 2-capable Starfighter was originally developed from combat experience in the Korean War, and its radical design emphasized high performance and speed. The combination of its long missile-like fuselage, big and powerful engine, and tiny, razor-sharp wings made for a very high-speed configuration. Some Starfighters served well into the 1990s, even though the first prototype flew as long ago as 1954.

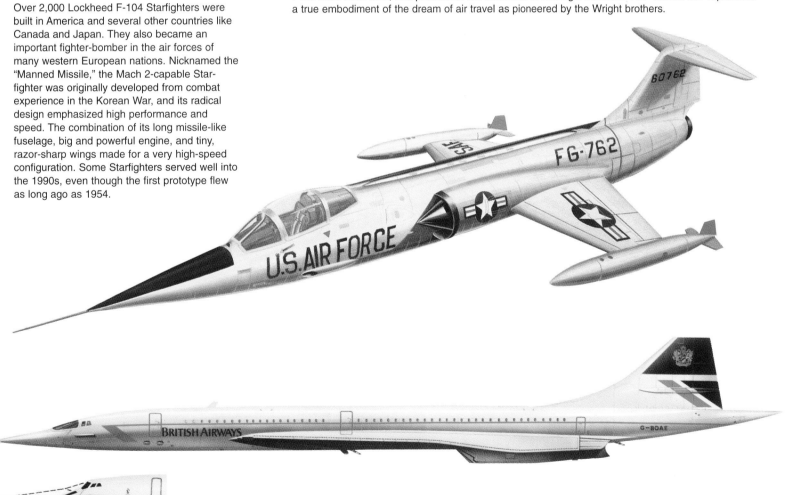

81. BAe/MCDONNELL DOUGLAS HARRIER

Bridging the gap between airplane and helicopter, the British Aerospace–McDonnell Douglas Harrier is a very special naval and ground-attack plane. Although the vertical takeoff and landing (V/TOL) concept had been around since the 1960s in the form of prototypes, the Harrier was the world's first successful production aircraft of this kind when it started flying in the 1970s. It is still in service today with the U.S. Marine Corps, the British military, and the air arms of several other friendly nations. The original versions were designed and built in Britain, but more recently the McDonnell Douglas company has engineered improved versions. The Harrier can land and take off vertically like a helicopter, but it can also fly like conventional aircraft because of thrust-vectoring technology. This consists of special rotating nozzles in the lower fuselage which direct the thrust of the engine. The nozzles point downward to give vertical control for landing and takeoff, and swivel to point rearward when the aircraft is flying straight and level to aim the engine's thrust to the rear (as in a conventional jet aircraft).

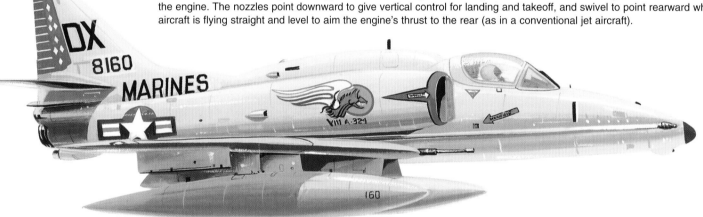

82. DOUGLAS A-4 SKYHAWK

The small, lightweight, and versatile A-4 Skyhawk first flew in 1954, and served very capably during the Vietnam War as an attack bomber with the U.S. Navy. A byproduct of Douglas Aircraft design group leader Ed Heinemann's philosophy, "Simplicate and Add Lightness," the A-4 with its relatively small wingspan did not have folded wings, unlike most other carrier aircraft. Without this feature the plane could be built with a lighter wing which, in turn, facilitated a much lighter aircraft. Almost 3,000 Skyhawks were built, and they operated not only with American forces—usually from aircraft carriers—but also with several foreign nations like Israel, Australia, and Argentina. Later Skyhawks could carry over 9,000 pounds of bombs and guided missiles under their fuselage and wings.

83. MIKOYAN-GUREVICH MiG-21 FISHBED

One of the most famous fighters of the 60s and 70s was Russia's high-performance MiG-21. This swift multi-role aircraft was built in larger numbers than any other jet fighter, with over 11,000 being built in several countries in a number of variations. Like their great rival the F-4 Phantom, MiG-21s have fought in many wars around the world, where their high speed and maneuverability have played a vital role. Some versions were specially designed to fly reconnaissance, while others were able to carry limited air-to-ground ordnance in addition to their air-to-air missiles. Many are still in service today, and special upgrade and modernization programmes have been devised to keep them in service in the future.

84. MCDONNELL DOUGLAS F-4 PHANTOM

The famous F-4 Phantom fighter and fighter-bomber was one of the most important fighters for the West for the entire post-World War II period. Over 5,000 were built for such U.S. allies as Great Britain, as well as for the USAF, Navy, and Marine Corps. The big and powerful twin-engined Phantom was able to fly at Mach 2-plus speed, and could carry up to 16,000 pounds of ordnance, including short- and medium-range air-to-air missiles, and guided missiles and bombs. Although the prototype first flew in 1958, some Phantoms are still in service today. In addition to fighter and fighter-bomber versions, there were reconnaissance Phantoms produced, as well as a model designed especially to attack enemy ground-radar installations. A legend in its own time, it was the most versatile aircraft used in the Vietnam War, singlehandedly destroying 145 MiGs.

85. DASSAULT MIRAGE III AND 2000

The Dassault company's best-selling family of Mirage delta-wing supersonic fighters and attack aircraft have brought immeasurable prestige to the French aviation industry for the past four decades. The Mirage III (above) was a versatile and effective interceptor, fighter, and tactical-support craft, designed to operate from small air strips. It was produced in large numbers for several different countries, and continued in service into the 1990s. Because of their special wing designs, Mirages are able to fly safely without a conventional horizontal tailplane. The more recent Mirage 2000 (below) is equipped with a special fly-by-wire control system that makes it even more agile than earlier models that were hampered by a lack of low-speed maneuverability. Some new versions, such as the Mirage 2000N, can carry nuclear weapons.

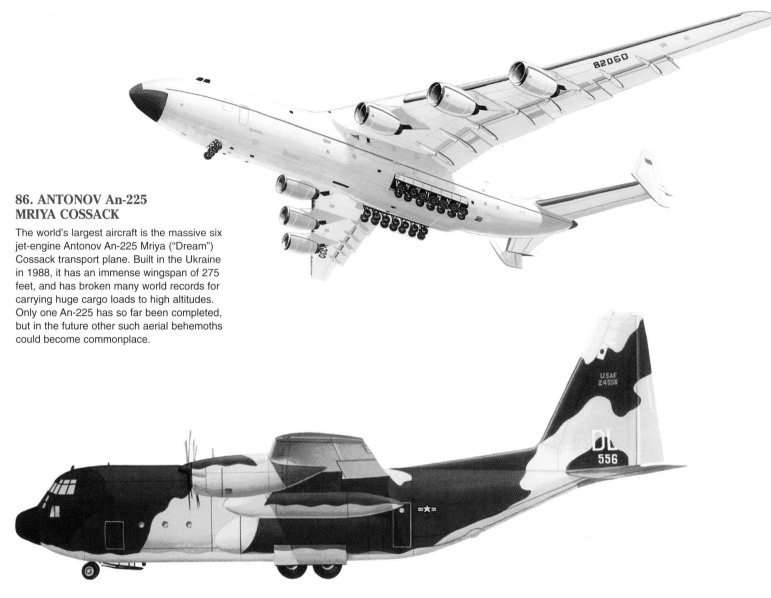

86. ANTONOV An-225 MRIYA COSSACK

The world's largest aircraft is the massive six jet-engine Antonov An-225 Mriya ("Dream") Cossack transport plane. Built in the Ukraine in 1988, it has an immense wingspan of 275 feet, and has broken many world records for carrying huge cargo loads to high altitudes. Only one An-225 has so far been completed, but in the future other such aerial behemoths could become commonplace.

87. LOCKHEED C-130 HERCULES

The most widely used military transport and cargo plane from the late 1950s up to the present day is the C-130 Hercules. This medium tactical transport plane made a name for itself during the Vietnam War, carrying large loads of military equipment, troops, and even light-armored vehicles to the battle zone. As of 1993, more than 2,000 Hercules have been produced for many customers, including the USAF and numerous foreign countries. Capable of a huge range of missions, special versions of this aircraft have been developed, including one that serves as an aerial gunship able to carry sideways-firing guns and cannons to attack ground targets.

88. SIKORSKY CH-53 JOLLY GREEN GIANT

One of the most powerful helicopters in military service, the mighty CH-53 can carry up to fifty-five troops in its spacious fuselage, as well as a large amount of cargo. The first CH-53 flew in 1964, and this important helicopter has operated under the name Sea Stallion with the U.S. Marine Corps as an assault and medium-lift machine. The USAF's versions of the CH-53 are nicknamed "Jolly Green Giants," and are usually employed for search-and-rescue missions, sometimes operating inside enemy territory to rescue downed airmen—a task they performed very well during the Vietnam War.

89. BOEING VERTOL CH-47 CHINOOK

One hero of the Vietnam War was the CH-47 Chinook, which carried troops and cargo for the U.S. Army. It first flew in 1961, and continues in service today with many air arms worldwide as a very capable heavy transport helicopter. Within its spacious fuselage, it can hold up to forty-four troops and assault weapons. The huge main rotor at each end of the fuselage gives the Chinook great stability, with this layout eliminating the need for the vertical tail rotor that is normally fitted to most other helicopters.

90. BOEING AH-64 APACHE

The best anti-tank helicopter ever developed is the superb AH-64 Apache. This champion among attack helicopters has already proven itself battleworthy in anti-armor missions carried out during the Gulf War. Today, even more powerful and capable versions are being built. The first Apaches entered service with the U.S. Army in the mid-1980s, and nowadays they also serve with the armies of several other countries, especially in the Middle East. The two-man crew are protected by armor plate, and the helicopter can carry up to sixteen anti-tank missiles under its stub wings. The Apache is equipped with a powerful "chain" gun mounted under its nose for attacking armored vehicles; and the newest models have mast-mounted Longbow radar to guide attack missiles into their targets, and locate enemy tanks even when they are hidden away.

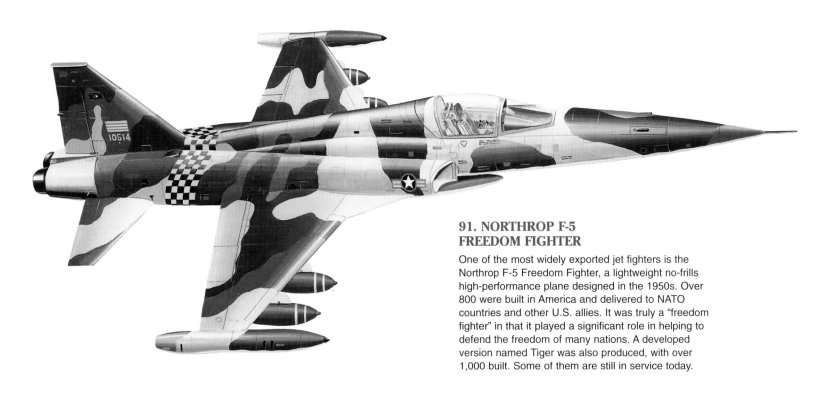

91. NORTHROP F-5 FREEDOM FIGHTER

One of the most widely exported jet fighters is the Northrop F-5 Freedom Fighter, a lightweight no-frills high-performance plane designed in the 1950s. Over 800 were built in America and delivered to NATO countries and other U.S. allies. It was truly a "freedom fighter" in that it played a significant role in helping to defend the freedom of many nations. A developed version named Tiger was also produced, with over 1,000 built. Some of them are still in service today.

92. GRUMMAN F-14 TOMCAT

The finest naval interceptor-fighter currently flying is the big twin-engined F-14 Tomcat. Operating from U.S. Navy aircraft carriers, Tomcats and the more recent Super Tomcats give vital air defense cover against enemy aircraft for the navy's ships and battle groups. F-14s have a particularly powerful radar system in the nose, and target enemy planes with very long-range Phoenix air-to-air missiles. Their "swing wings" allow them to land at slow speed on an aircraft carrier with the wings extended; but when the wings are swept back, the Tomcat has an exciting high-speed performance of over Mach 2. The pilot is accompanied on board by a "back-seater" who tends to the radar operation and aiming the weapons.

93. MIKOYAN-GUREVICH MiG-29 FULCRUM

The very capable MiG-29 fighter has excellent maneuverability and air-to-air weapon-carrying capability, and has been built in large numbers for Russia's air force and its allies. Developed to replace a wide array of older fighter types, MiG-29s have been in service from the mid-1980s up to the present day. One of the special features of this large aircraft is its ability to operate from primitive airfields where the soft or rough ground would normally prove a hazard for most other modern jet fighters.

94. LOCKHEED SR-71 BLACKBIRD

The fastest-ever production aircraft is the remarkable Lockheed SR-71 Blackbird. Developed in great secrecy during the 1960s by the renowned Lockheed "Skunk Works" design shop, the Blackbird is an ultra high-speed, high-altitude reconnaissance aircraft. With 21st century looks and performance, the unique blended shape of the plane's structure gives it the ability to fly at high speed, while the airframe itself is partially made from titanium—a special metal that is very strong, light, and corrosion-and temperature-resistant. No other production airplane can match the Blackbird's cruising speed of around Mach 3. Recently, some Blackbirds have been used on special reconnaissance and research missions by the National Aeronautics and Space Administration (NASA).

95. BOEING/MCDONNELL DOUGLAS F-15 EAGLE

The greatest air superiority fighter currently in service, the magnificent F-15 Eagle has served with the USAF since 1974, and has performed brilliantly during air battles in a number of wars. The main fighter versions of the Eagle carry an impressive array of air-to-air missiles, and a special fighter-bomber derivative can hold a wide selection of air-to-ground bombs and missiles. Eagles have been exported to friendly countries like Japan, where some of them have been built under license. They have been deployed in all the major conflicts of recent years, and were especially effective in air-to-air combat during the 1990–91 Gulf War. In the standard fighter models of the F-15 there is just the single pilot, but the special fighter-bomber variant is designed for two crew members, with the "back-seater" dealing with all the navigation and weapon-aiming tasks for the air-to-ground weapons. Some F-15s are even able to carry nuclear bombs.

96. GENERAL DYNAMICS F-16 FIGHTING FALCON

The most widely produced jet fighter on an international scale is the F-16 Fighting Falcon. Defender of the western world, this aircraft flies for many foreign air forces in addition to having several hundred in service with the USAF. Designed in the 1970s by General Dynamics and first flown in 1974, the F-16 is still produced today by Lockheed Martin—a tribute to its pre-eminence. So far, over 4,000 have been built mostly in the United States, but with a large number constructed in foreign countries under license. Many European, Asian, and Middle Eastern countries now fly the F-16. A multi-role fighter, it is able to dogfight brilliantly because of its excellent maneuverability. In addition to air-to-air missiles, the Fighting Falcon can also carry a wide range of weapons for ground attack. Its superbly blended wing and fuselage shape allows for efficient air flow over the whole plane, and its powerful single turbofan engine gives it a top speed of around Mach 2. F-16s have been flown successfully in several air wars; and in the hands of a skilled pilot, the agile and powerful Fighting Falcon is almost invincible.

97. SUKHOI Su-27 FLANKER

Sukhoi's outstanding Su-27 Flanker demonstrates how far fighter technology has progressed from the wood, wire, and canvas biplanes of the First World War. This Russian air superiority multi-role fighter has two huge turbofan jet engines that can propel it to speeds of over Mach 2, and a cleverly designed blended fuselage and wing shape which—together with special fly-by-wire controls—gives it great speed and maneuverability. It can carry several large air-to-air missiles, and has a powerful nose-mounted radar system that detects targets at long distances. Russian air force Flankers have become famous for their special dogfighting maneuvers in which the plane suddenly rises vertically and almost hovers before returning to the dogfight. This tactic gives the Russian pilot a strategic edge over his opponent.

98. MIL Mi-24 HIND

Russia's big and impressive Mil Mi-24 attack helicopter—nicknamed "Hind" in the West— is a real flying gunship with rockets, guns, and anti-tank missiles on pylons under its stub wings, and a powerful gun in its special under-nose turret. Its main job is to attack enemy tanks and other military vehicles. The Mi-24 is also an assault helicopter because of its unique ability to carry eight armed troops to the frontlines in the central compartment of its fuselage.

99. BOEING/MCDONNELL DOUGLAS F/A-18 HORNET

The Hornet was designed as a multi-role combat aircraft able to carry out fighter missions and drop bombs accurately. It was developed primarily as a carrier-borne naval fighter and fighter-bomber that can hold about 15,500 pounds of bombs and guided weapons. The Hornet performed very effectively during the Gulf War against Iraq, and currently serves with the U.S. Navy and Marine Corps. It has also been built for several friendly countries around the world.

100. NORTHROP GRUMMAN B-2 SPIRIT

Is this the shape of things to come? The most advanced warplane in the sky right now is the Northrop Grumman B-2 Spirit. It is a strategic bomber that has operated with the USAF since the mid-1990s, and can carry nuclear weapons or a huge bombload of about 50,000 pounds. The B-2's unique flying-wing layout—pioneered by Jack Northrop during the 1940s—and the use of radiation-absorbent materials in its construction, allows it to almost completely evade radar detection. In the future, most warplanes will be engineered according to the imperatives of this "stealth technology," which will undoubtedly fill the skies with even more interesting and unusual aircraft designs.

Index

(The number following each plane refers to its caption number.)

Background Illustration: Cutaway of Martin B-57 (ENGLISH ELECTRIC CANBERRA) (plane no. 66)